YOUTH WITH ASPERGER'S
SYNDROME

A Different
Drummer

HELPING YOUTH WITH MENTAL, PHYSICAL, AND SOCIAL CHALLENGES

Title List

YOUTH WITH ASPERGER'S SYNDROME

A Different Drummer

by Zachary Chastain
and Phyllis Livingston

Mason Crest Publishers
Philadelphia

Mason Crest Publishers Inc.
370 Reed Road
Broomall, Pennsylvania 19008
(866) MCP-BOOK (toll free)
www.masoncrest.com

First printing

1 2 3 4 5 6 7 8 9 10

ISBN 978-1-4222-0133-6 (series)

Library of Congress Cataloging-in-Publication Data

Chastain, Zachary.
  Youth with Asperger's syndrome : a different drummer / by Zachary Chastain and Phyllis Livingston.
      p. cm. — (Helping youth with mental, physical, and social challenges)
  Includes bibliographical references and index.
  ISBN-13: 978-1-4222-0137-4
  1. Asperger's syndrome in adolescence—Juvenile literature. I. Livingston, Phyllis, 1957– II. Title.
RJ506.A9.C44 2008
618.92'85882—dc22
2006026370

Interior pages produced by
Harding House Publishing Service, Inc.
www.hardinghousepages.com
Interior design by MK Bassett-Harvey.
Cover design by MK Bassett-Harvey.
Cover Illustration by Keith Rosko.
Printed in the Hashemite Kingdom of Jordan.

The creators of this book have made every effort to provide accurate information, but it should not be used as a substitute for the help and services of trained professionals.

Contents

Introduction

We are all people first, before anything else. Our shared humanity is more important than the impressions we give to each other by how we look, how we learn, or how we act. Each of us is worthy simply because we are all part of the human race. Though we are all different in many ways, we can celebrate our differences as well as our similarities.

In this book series, you will read about many young people with various special needs that impact their lives in different ways. The disabilities are not *who* the people are, but the disabilities are an important characteristic of each person. When we recognize that we all have differing needs, we can grow toward greater awareness and tolerance of each other. Just as important, we can learn to accept our differences.

Not all young people with a disability are the same as the persons in the stories. But you will learn from these stories how a special need impacts a young person, as well as his or her family and friends. The story will help you understand differences better and appreciate how differences make us all stronger and better.

—*Cindy Croft, M.A.Ed.*

Did you know that as many as 8 percent of teens experience anxiety or depression, and as many as 70 to 90 percent will use substances such as alcohol or illicit drugs at some time? Other young people are living with life-threatening diseases including HIV infection and cancer, as well as chronic psychiatric conditions such as bipolar disease and schizophrenia. Still other teens have the challenge of being "different" from peers because they are intellectually gifted, are from another culture, or have trouble controlling their behavior or socializing with others. All youth with challenges experience additional stresses compared to their typical peers. The good news is that there are many resources and supports available to help these young people, as well as their friends and families.

The stories contained in each book of this series also contain factual information that will enhance your own understanding of the particular condition being presented. If you or someone you know is struggling with a similar condition or experience, this series can give you important information about where and how you can get help. After reading these stories, we hope that you will be more open to the differences you encounter in your peers and more willing to get to know others who are "different."
—*Carolyn Bridgemohan, M.D.*

Chapter 1
Gerbils and Lions

Duncan had always loved to sing. Even when he was a little kid, only six years old, he'd taught himself to reach up to the record player and place the needle onto his parents' old jazz albums. His parents used to brag to their friends about their son, the musical prodigy, who knew every lyric in their vinyl collection. Duncan could sing along with Ella Fitzgerald and Nat "King" Cole, and he had an advanced vocabulary by the time most kids were struggling to form whole sentences.

But something was missing. Even the way Duncan sang seemed strangely wrong; the notes were too perfect, too rhythmic. If someone had asked Duncan's parents, they would have said his singing lacked "personality"—but certainly not precision.

Duncan didn't play with the other kids. He was happy in the corner of the playroom, headphones on his ears. When he did talk to the other kids, it was five, ten, even fifteen minutes of nonstop Duncan-monologue. Before Duncan could finish telling the little boy in blue sneakers across from him how many tracks were on Louis Armstrong's fourth album, the little boy started crying or left the room.

Duncan was nine years old when he punched his fourth-grade music teacher, Mr. Thomas, in the face. Duncan's family already knew something was wrong, but this accelerated the process of getting him professional help. Earlier in elementary school, Duncan's teachers and doctors thought he had attention-deficit/hyperactivity disorder (ADHD), or maybe oppositional defiant disorder (ODD). They had prescribed drugs to treat the ADHD and ODD, but they ignored—until that day in fourth grade—the underlying issues that were causing his in-school conflicts.

Duncan was frequently scolded for rudely correcting teachers and peers during class, even though he was often right. Then, when Mr. Thomas had refused to admit a musical mistake, Duncan's fury mounted through class. During the piano portion of class, the teacher tried to move Duncan's hand to a different note on the keyboard, but Duncan recoiled. He flung his fist backward, landing it squarely on Mr. Thomas's nose. Mr. Thomas gave a scream of pain; blood gushed out; and amid all the chaos that followed,

Duncan played the *correct* notes on the piano, the ones he'd wanted to play all along.

By the fifth grade, Duncan's Asperger's syndrome was diagnosed by both the school psychologist and Duncan's family psychiatrist. These professionals explained to Duncan's parents that his inability to make and keep friends was a result of his AS. They explained that Duncan's hyperactivity was a symptom of his "obsessive" area of interest—at that time, it was music and trains. They told Duncan's family and his teachers that his outbursts of anger were due largely to a lack of social ability, not ODD.

In the sixth grade, Duncan entered the treacherous terrain of middle school with naive hopes for a second chance. It wasn't long before his hopes were shattered. On his first day of gym class, during a game of volleyball, Duncan exploded at Mrs. Ames, the physical education teacher. She had not yet been briefed on Duncan's condition, and she repeatedly scolded him for breaking the rules, like staying within his zone and giving others room to play. Eventually, the pressure built up, and Duncan started screaming at Mrs. Ames to leave him alone. As he sat in the main office waiting to see the principal, he knew it was all over: any chance at a new start was gone, just like that.

The next day he walked to his locker with his head down. He could already hear whispers and sense fingers pointing at his back. He was once again "the psycho"—a title he hadn't heard since he punched Mr. Thomas. Lately, he'd heard teachers call him the "ticking time bomb"; he knew both teachers and students disliked him. Other children saw him as mean, arrogant, and awkward. Teachers who didn't know Duncan well weren't informed of Duncan's condition, and they often considered him a "problem child" or a "poor performer."

In middle school, Duncan was punished more than ever for not fitting in. He kept singing, but only on his own; he didn't dare audition for chorus or musical theater. Without an understanding of social cues, he was doomed to loneliness and depression.

Those years seemed to drag on forever, but soon enough the last summer days of August were approaching, and high school was just a few weeks away. Duncan was profoundly indifferent to the upcoming school year. His middle school years had hardened his heart.

He had achieved what he wanted, but at a price. He was no longer "the psycho" but simply a silent ghost. He had learned that silence was a language in itself; and if he couldn't speak everyone else's, then he would fade into the background. The school didn't seem to object. In seventh and eighth grade, Duncan's teachers had allowed him to take his work to the special education room, where he could do his work unbothered and eat his lunch alone. If high school meant anything to Duncan, it meant his safety would be threatened. High school was a new world, unknown and mysterious, where anything could happen.

"It's kind of like Asperger's is a parrot that sits on your shoulder," his older brother Ryan had told him once.

Ryan was entering his senior year of high school as Duncan entered his freshman year. Ryan was always trying to find different analogies and metaphors to help Duncan, or at least make him laugh, but Duncan didn't do well with metaphors. He preferred concise, straightforward language. Still, he appreciated his older brother's attempts, especially since his mom and dad preferred to stay at a safe distance. He knew they loved him, but they were always so busy. They paid for social-training sessions every Wednesday morning; they signed the right paperwork so Duncan had special consideration at school; they found a professional therapist for Duncan. But Duncan didn't want to talk to a professional. He would have much rather talked to his parents.

"High school's a whole new animal," Ryan told him, "but don't you worry. You've just got to learn to tame the new beast."

Duncan stared at Ryan blankly. "What kind of animal was middle school?" he asked, finally realizing that Ryan was speaking in metaphors again.

"Middle school was a gerbil, Duncan, and high school is a lion."

Duncan didn't understand. "But statistically, aren't gerbils much more dangerous than lions? Gerbils are both common household pets and carriers of Tyzzer's disease, which can infect open wounds on humans. Lions, on the other hand, are isolated to remote regions of Africa, where little exposure to humans is possible."

Ryan grinned. "True, Duncan. So I guess high school is more like a Tyzzer's disease–carrying gerbil, and middle school is a ferocious lion. Sorry I switched the two."

Duncan didn't understand why his brother was laughing. "That's all right," he said, accepting his brother's apology literally.

After the first day of school, Ryan stopped by Duncan's room. "See what I mean—it's dangerous out there, like a disease-infested gerbil. But gerbils can be tamed. You just need a wheel."

Duncan shook his head. "I don't know. The high school is so much faster and bigger. But I'll be all right. I guess."

"You sure will," Ryan reassured him, "and you can eat lunch with me and my friends any day you want. And I'll introduce you to some people Wednesday, after school, at the Trekky meeting."

"Thanks, Ryan."

Ryan started to leave the room, but Duncan stopped him. "Ryan. . ."

"Yeah?" Duncan paused in the doorway.

"There's this girl." Duncan struggled to find the words he was seeking.

"A girl?" Ryan grinned. "Already?"

"Yeah. Her name's Sarah Alewine."

"Oh yeah! She's into physics, right? Sophomore?"

"Yeah. What should I do?"

Ryan thought for a moment. The truth was, Duncan knew, Ryan didn't talk to many girls either.

Besides being his only brother, Ryan was also Duncan's only friend, one of the few people who took almost as much interest in physics, science fiction, and computer-gaming as Duncan did. Ryan was proud to be a "geek" and a very social person at the same time—but only within a close-knit group of friends.

"Well," Ryan said, "you have to ask her to the movies, of course. I mean, that is the obvious first move."

"Oh, right—the movies. Yeah, I'll do that."

As a brother who had lived with Duncan's AS for fifteen years, Ryan should have known better: Duncan almost always took advice literally, with few second thoughts. Exactly one week later, Duncan was sitting in first period physics, clutching two movie tickets in his sweaty palm.

What Is Asperger's Syndrome?

Asperger's syndrome, which is sometimes called autistic psychopathy, is often thought of as a form of high-functioning autism. Asperger's syndrome belongs to a group of childhood disorders known as *pervasive* developmental disorders (PDDs) or autistic *spectrum* disorders. These disorders are characterized by delays in the development of multiple basic functions, including *socialization* and communication. Parents often notice symptoms of PDD as early as infancy; typically, the onset of symptoms occurs before a child is three years old. PDDs are not fatal, and they do not affect normal life expectancy. (However, an increased risk of suicide is associated with Asperger's syndrome.)

The symptoms of a PDD include communication problems such as:

- difficulty using and understanding language
- difficulty relating to people, objects, and events
- unusual play with toys and other objects
- difficulty with changes in routine or familiar surroundings
- repetitive body movements or behavior patterns

Children with PDD vary widely in abilities, intelligence, and behavior. Some children do not speak at all, while others speak in limited phrases

Symptoms of a pervasive developmental disorder such as Asperger's syndrome will typically appear before a child is three years old, and may include difficulty relating to people, objects, and events.

Because all young children have limited social skills and vary in development of communication skills, some doctors will wait until the child is older to make a specific diagnosis.

or conversations; still others have relatively normal language development. Repetitive play skills and limited social skills are generally common to all children with a PDD. Unusual responses to sensory information, such as loud noises or sudden bright lights, are also common. Autism, Asperger's syndrome, Rett syndrome, childhood disintegrative disorder, and PDD not otherwise specified (PDD-NOS) are all types of PDD.

Some clinicians use PDD-NOS as a "temporary" diagnosis for children under the age of five. The main reason for waiting to offer a more specific diagnosis is that all very young children have limited social interaction and communication skills, which means it can be difficult to diagnose the severity of a disorder. Some children may take longer to learn specific skills, and some behaviors may be outgrown. By age five, however, unusual behaviors will either resolve or develop into a disorder that can be definitively labeled.

PDD has no known cure, although medications are used to address certain behavioral problems. Therapy for children with PDD should be specialized according to the child's specific needs. Some children with PDD benefit from special classrooms where the class size is small enough that instruction is given on a one-to-one basis. Other children with these disorders function well in standard special education classes or even in regular classes with support. Early intervention including appropriate and specialized educational programs and support services plays a critical role in improving the outcome of individuals with PDD.

Autism is the PDD that has been studied the most, and it is the most well-known in the general public. (Movies such as *Rain Man* have helped make this disorder famous; however, there are still many commonly held misconceptions about autism.)

Experts generally agree that no single condition called autism exists. Instead, there is a spectrum of autistic conditions, with different forms of autism falling at different positions on this spectrum. Researchers are not certain, however, how this spectrum should be divided. Some possible divisions include:

- autistics who speak versus those who do not
- autistics with *seizures* versus those without
- autistics with more *stereotypical behaviors* versus those with fewer

Some researchers are trying to identify the genetic material associated with these traits as a way to make logical groupings. Eventually, one may hear autistics described as being with or without a specific gene or with or without changes to a certain *chromosome*.

Autism is a behavior disorder characterized by impaired social communication, social interaction, and social imagination. Those with autism often have a restricted range of interests and display repetitive mannerisms, along with altered reactions to the everyday environment.

Autism was first described in 1943 by an American physician named Leo Kanner. Although the

While some children with a PDD will do well in a regular classroom setting, others will benefit more from the one-on-one attention of a small special education class.

condition undoubtedly existed long before Kanner, he was the one who coined the term "autism." His research, however, did not receive much attention in the medical community, and children with autistic symptoms continued to be incorrectly diagnosed with childhood schizophrenia.

Children with autism can often not be identified until they are at least two years old, when they fail to learn to speak and understand language as quickly as other toddlers their age. When they do use words, they may use them in peculiar ways, such as echoing words in a parrot-like manner. Frequently, they do not look up when their own names are called, and they fail to pick up on others' moods from expressions and other nonverbal forms of communication. Children with autism are unlikely to "pretend"—and if they do, they are more apt to pretend to be a car than a doctor, a washing machine than a mommy or daddy. By the time these children are in school, their inability to play with other children often alerts teachers to their disorder. They may be mute, or they may use odd or inappropriate words that fail to communicate much of anything.

Four times as many males as females have autism, but studies show that the incidence of autism is increasing: in 1966, four to five babies per 10,000 births developed this disorder, while in 2003, between fourteen and thirty-nine babies per 10,000 developed autism. Some people believe that something in our environment is causing this increase, while others argue that heightened awareness of this disorder in

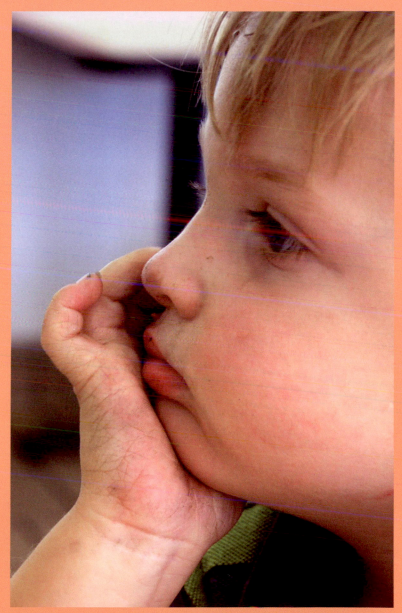

More males than females are diagnosed with autism. However, the overall incidence of autism has been increasing, from four to five babies per 10,000 in 1966 to 14 to 39 per 10,000 in 2003.

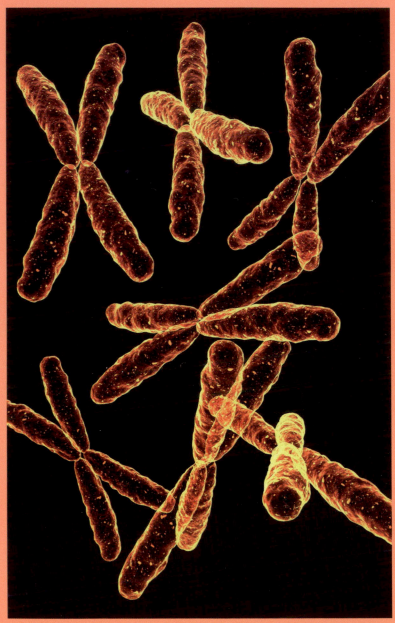

Changes to multiple genes may cause autism. Genes are packets of DNA found on chromosomes within the nuclei of cells.

both the medical community and the general public has simply led to more diagnoses.

Autism is defined by behaviors—but it is caused by *organic* or genetic (rather than psychological) factors. Organic causes include:

- prenatal problems such as maternal rubella (measles) infection

- untreated *metabolic disorders*

- anticonvulsants taken by the mother during pregnancy

- postnatal infections such as *encephalitis*

Multiple genes may also be involved with autism; studies indicate that the likely candidates are chromosomes 2, 7, 15, 16, and 19.

The common symptoms of autism usually appear within the first three years of life. These include:

- absence or impairment of imaginative and social play

- impaired ability to make friends

- impaired ability to have a sustained conversation with others

- stereotyped, repetitive, or unusual language

- restricted patterns of interest that are abnormal in intensity or focus

- inflexible adherence to specific routines or rituals

- preoccupation with parts of objects (rather than the whole)

Children with some symptoms of autism—but not enough to be considered eligible for diagnosis of the classical form of the disorder—are often diagnosed with PDD-NOS. Children who appear normal for their first seven years of life and then begin to lose skills and show autistic behaviors may be diagnosed with childhood disintegrative disorder. Girls with autistic behaviors accompanied by inadequate brain growth,

Individuals with Asperger's in general have above average intelligence, but poorly developed social skills. Therefore, the child that seems slow or withdrawn may just have difficulty interacting with others.

seizures, and other **neurological** problems are usually considered to have Rett syndrome. People with autistic behavior but well-developed language skills are usually diagnosed with Asperger's syndrome.

In very broad terms, individuals with Asperger's have normal or above average intelligence, and **atypical** or poorly developed social skills. As a result, emotional and social development usually happens later than usual.

The Latest Research: Asperger's and Hearing

Children with Asperger's syndrome often have difficulty understanding others' speech in surroundings where there is background noise or talking. Researchers from Cambridge University in the United Kingdom, Alcantra and his colleagues, wanted to verify the validity of these reports, to quantify the difficulties these individual have in hearing others, and to better understand why this occurs.

The researchers measured speech reception thresholds (SRTs), defined as speech-to-noise ratio at which approximately 50 percent of the speech is recognized, in eleven individuals with high-functioning autism/Asperger's syndrome (with an average age of twenty-one), and nine age-matched, normal-hearing **control** individuals (with an average age of nineteen). Inside a chamber designed to generate measurable background noise or speech, individuals listened to sentences spoken by a British male speaker; the speech was accompanied by four different types of background sounds.

The researchers confirmed that the SRTs for the Asperger's group were worse than the controls', meaning those with Asperger's syndrome had a more difficult time identifying the voice with different background noises than did the controls. Specifically, when the background noises had "dips" or pauses in them, as speech naturally does, controls were able

Another factor contributing to the delayed social skill development may be that individuals with Asperger's syndrome have trouble hearing and understanding speech if there is any background noise.

to more easily recognize the voice than those with Asperger's syndrome could. In other words, to fully hear and recognize the voice, the Asperger's group needed a higher signal-to-noise ratio whenever there were dips in the background sound.

These results suggest that individuals with Asperger's have real and measurable problems understanding speech when there is background noise. The researchers hypothesized that this was likely because the individuals' ability to obtain information about the speech present during the dips in the background noise was reduced by a failure to fully integrate information in the brain from glimpses of the voice during temporary dips in the background noise.

Why does this matter? Because if people with Asperger's can't clearly process speech in a variety of noisy social settings, their social development and interactions are likely to be further impaired. Teachers, parents, and therapists who understand this characteristic of individuals with Asperger's will be better able to help these individuals compensate for their challenges.

Chapter 2
Every Thorn Has a Rose

The film was called *Every Thorn Has a Rose*, which, for Duncan, would normally have been reason enough not to go see it. But he'd never been more excited about a film in his life. In the middle of a full classroom, Duncan was shaking all over, hoping no one noticed.

He was thinking about the last few weeks: he hated high school, but he loved listening to Sarah Alewine talk to her friend between third and fourth periods. High school was horrible. It had all the boredom of middle school, but none of the safe places and routines that he had found by his third year of middle school. Duncan rarely enjoyed change; he thought of it as unproductive and bothersome. The only change he liked was Sarah, who was like magic: a year older than Duncan, well liked by everyone in her class, an excellent physicist, and—most important from Duncan's perspective—an excellent actor and singer. Duncan was the only freshman in AP physics, and he sat in the back of the room. From there, he watched Sarah Alewine (who sat in the front row) raise her hand for all the toughest questions.

Duncan knew all about Sarah. In his small town, information wasn't difficult to come by, but Duncan knew more than just Sarah's address. His locker was near her friend Lacey's locker, where she often stopped between third and fourth periods. For those three minutes between classes, he'd pretend to fumble around for a pencil buried at the bottom of his locker, listening to Sarah and Lacey talk. Some days the information was quite valuable—he learned she liked strawberry ice cream (which was also his favorite)—and some days it was useless—he learned she did not like bug bites (but who did, after all?).

The information Duncan needed most came earlier that week, when he heard Lacey and Sarah talk about a movie being released the upcoming Friday night. Sarah wanted to see it because it starred George Clooney as an assassin. And so, that same night, Duncan went to work. Sitting at his computer (which he had bought with his own money and dubbed "Lady Ella" after his favorite jazz singer), Duncan prepared for the first date of his life. He bought tickets, found and printed online maps of nearby parks, and then chose a perfect spot by the park's waterfront, where he imagined he would hold Sarah's hand (although he told himself not to press his luck). The only thing left undone, of course, was asking Sarah to join him on this night out.

That night, Duncan remained at his computer for another hour. He googled dozens of George Clooney pictures, comparing himself to the man Sarah seemed so interested in. Duncan poked at his cheekbones in the mirror; they didn't look anything like Clooney's. And it would be at least another fifteen years before he could grow pepper-gray hair. That was the biggest problem: George Clooney was not a young, hip actor, but rather an older, more seasoned man. This presented little hope for Duncan, the underclassman, who stood barely five feet six inches tall.

Duncan was nervous about asking Sarah, but it never occurred to him that she might not say yes. He didn't understand the social cues and unspoken rules surrounding high school dating. Duncan knew he didn't understand girls anymore than he understood anyone else in the world, but he wanted to understand Sarah. Because conversations with his peers were few, Duncan placed the people he met into two categories: those who were intelligent and those who were not. Sarah, he had decided, was not only intelligent, but beautiful, and that was enough for him. Friday morning, he would ask her on a date.

When that morning finally arrived, after a week of planning and a month of dreaming, Duncan found he was more than anxious for class to end, so he could execute his plan.

The sophomore at the desk next to Duncan was rapping his pencil against his desk: *tap, tap, tap*. It was as if the pencil was a drumstick, rapping out against the metal rim of a snare. Duncan looked around the room to see if anyone else noticed the piercing noise, but everyone seemed calm, eyes fixed on Mr. Funk, who was getting excited about a circular motion equation.

TAP, TAP, TAP.

The noise persisted, becoming louder and louder, a drill into the side of Duncan's head. He began to look for an escape—the bathroom, the hallway, anywhere but near this violent tapping—but he couldn't leave now, not with class almost over. He needed to catch Sarah immediately after class ended; that was the plan. He had to keep it together.

TAP! TAP! TAP!

Duncan began taking slow, controlled breaths, recalling what they had taught him to do in elementary school, when doctors first diagnosed him with AS. *This is just part of AS*, he thought. *You're just sensitive to the repetition of auditory noises*, he continued to rationalize, desperately trying to calm himself.

TAP! TAP! TAP!

Duncan put both hands to his ears in agony. *PLEASE MAKE IT STOP*, he pleaded inside his head to no one in particular. And then he glanced at the boy with the pencil, and it all became clear: Josh Arnsdale, the sophomore Duncan had seen talking to Sarah on numerous occasions at lunch and after school. *Of course*, Duncan thought, *he knows about my plans with Sarah and wants to sabotage them.*

Duncan shifted in his seat and said, "Josh, can you stop pounding your pencil on your desk, please?"

A few heads turned around in the front of the class.

"No need to scream, man" said Josh. "I didn't even know I was tapping it."

"What you do mean, stop screaming?" Duncan was speaking loud enough that the entire class was staring by now. Suddenly, everything was too loud, not just the pencil. Duncan was overwhelmed by the sound of his own heartbeat, thudding in his ears, and the beginnings of quiet laughter from a few girls up front, maybe even from Sarah.

Mr. Funk made his way toward the back of the room, where Duncan was sweating and trying to concentrate on making his hands stop shaking, afraid he'd rip the two tickets. "What's the problem here, Josh?" Mr. Funk asked.

"No problem, Mr. Funk—I was just tapping my pencil and Duncan freaked out."

"Just tapping your pencil?" Mr. Funk repeated.

"Yeah, like this." Josh demonstrated: *TAP! TAP! TAP!*

That was all it took. Duncan shot up with a shout, and ran out of the classroom and into the hallway.

He could feel tears forming as the bell rang for class to end. *Just my luck*, he thought. *Now everything is ruined. I blew it. I blew it.* He felt trapped, as though everyone back in class knew something he didn't know. At the same time, he knew what he had just experienced back there would never be explained or understood.

As the class filed out of the classroom, Duncan waited down the hall, averting his gaze until they had all left, so he could go back and get his backpack. And then he felt a hand on his shoulder. When he turned around, his breath caught halfway between lungs and mouth. It was Sarah, looking concerned but not frightened.

"What happened in there?" she asked.

Duncan looked at her in silent disbelief.

She smiled at him. "I can't stand pencil-tapping either, honestly. It just gets inside my head. I can't concentrate."

He tried to respond, but he was frozen, unable to stutter out a single word. All his carefully prepared speeches and impressive facts about physics and theater were locked under a sheet of ice, unreachable. She was still smiling, though, waiting for him to say something.

This is not the plan, Duncan thought. *This isn't how it's supposed to work.* "I'm sorry," he blurted and shoved the tickets into her hand. "Just take these and bring your friend

Lacey. I hope Clooney is cool." He almost ran down the hall away from her. *Idiot*, he was thinking. *Idiot!*

From behind him, he heard her say, "Wait a minute." He slowed down. "You didn't want to go on a date with me tonight, did you?"

Duncan's heart stopped.

"Because I don't date guys I don't know."

He turned around to face her; after all, he had nothing to lose now.

"But I saw you checking out the theater poster outside the auditorium," Sarah continued, "and I think you should come to the theater meeting next Monday—if you're interested, I mean. And if you are, you should try out for the play on Wednesday, because I've heard you sing, and I think your voice is perfect for the lead role. We could talk then. We'll talk, and then we'll know each other, and you can ask me out next Friday."

Duncan was baffled, but he knew enough to say, "Okay."

"Great." She smiled at him again. "Because I only go on dates with guys I know. So I'll see you Monday. And Wednesday, I hope."

"Yeah, I'll see you then."

"Okay. Bye, Duncan."

He walked away stunned, but elated. *How does she even know my name?*

What Does Asperger's Syndrome Look Like?

A person with Asperger's demonstrates:

- severe social interaction impairment, particularly when it comes to reciprocating and *empathizing* with others' feelings

- difficulties interpreting nonverbal communications

- peculiar speech habits that include repeating words or phrases and a flat, emotionless vocal tone

- an apparent lack of "common sense"

- a fascination with obscure or limited subjects (for example, the parts of a clock or small machine, railroad schedules, astronomical data, etc.), often to the exclusion of other interests

- clumsy and awkward physical movements

- odd or eccentric behaviors (hand wringing or finger flapping; swaying or other repetitious whole-body movements; watching spinning objects for long periods of time).

Children with Asperger's learn to talk at the usual age and often have above-average verbal skills in some ways. They also have normal or above-normal intelligence and the ability to feed or dress themselves and take care of their daily needs.

Some clinicians believe that communicative or *cognitive* deficiencies are so essential to the concept

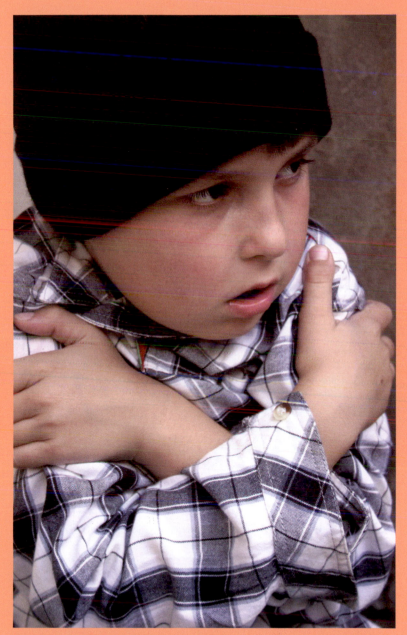

Because children with Asperger's have difficulty understanding others' feelings, their social interactions are impaired.

of autism that Asperger's should be considered a completely separate condition from autism. Most experts, however, do not believe that a dividing line can be drawn between "high-functioning" autism and Asperger's.

Most children with Asperger's are diagnosed during the elementary school years because the symptoms of the disorder become more apparent at this point. These symptoms include:

- Poor pragmatic language skills. This phrase means that the child does not use the right tone or volume of voice for a specific context, and does not understand that using humorous or slang expressions also depends on social context.

- Problems with hand-eye coordination and other visual skills.

- Problems making eye contact with others.

- Learning difficulties, which may range from mild to severe.

- A tendency to become absorbed in a particular topic and not know when others are bored with conversation about it. At this stage in their education, children with Asperger's syndrome are likely to be labeled as "nerds."

- Repetitive behaviors. These include such behaviors as counting a group of coins or marbles over and over, reciting the same song or poem several times, and buttoning and unbuttoning a jacket repeatedly.

Adolescence is one of the most painful periods of life for young people with Asperger's, because social interactions are more complex in this age group and require more subtle social skills. Some boys with Asperger's syndrome become frustrated trying to relate to their peers and may become aggressive. Both boys and girls with the disorder are often **naive** for their age, which makes them easily manipulated by their classmates. They are also more vulnerable than most youngsters to peer pressure.

Children with Asperger's are often diagnosed in elementary school, when symptoms such as difficulty making eye contact become apparent.

Adolescents with Asperger's are often more naive that their peers.
This leaves them vulnerable to teasing and peer pressure.

Mind-Blind

While people who are not autistic are constantly picking up on clues about other people's emotional states, people with Asperger syndrome have a condition that's sometimes called "mind-blindness." They lack the natural ability to see the subtexts of social interaction; in other words, they can't "read between the lines." They may interpret figures of speech literally; in some ways, they are a lot like the character named Data on *Star Trek: The Next Generation.*

This often results in them making well-meaning remarks that may offend. They lack a sense of what is acceptable in polite conversation. They also tend to lack the ability to broadcast their own emotional state with their body language, facial expressions, and vocal tone. This doesn't mean they necessarily don't have emotions (as was the case with Data on *Star Trek*); some people with Asperger's may have very strong feelings, but lack the ability to express them. Others, however, do have reduced levels of emotion.

Some individuals with Asperger's syndrome are unable to make eye contact with others; they find such contact too overwhelming. Others, however, demonstrate just the opposite behavior: unblinking, staring eye contact that makes other people uncomfortable. In the same way, people with Asperger's may use absolutely no gestures when they're speaking—or they may use exaggerated and inappropriate gestures.

Like Data, many people with Asperger's syndrome use their intelligence to learn more acceptable

People with Asperger's may seem strange and robotic when talking with others because they tend to take words literally instead of grasping the underlying meaning.

behaviors that allow them to blend in with others. They intellectually learn the social skills that come naturally to others.

Narrow and Intense Interests

Asperger's syndrome can involve an intense and obsessive level of focus on the things that interest the individual. For example, one person might be obsessed with baseball stats, another with obscure geographical facts for every nation of the world, or another with building tiny models of ships. Children with Asperger's are particularly apt to be interested in means of transportation (such as trains), computers, mathematics, dinosaurs, astronomy, and geography. All children may have some degree of interest in many of these topics, but the difference with Asperger children is the unusual intensity of their interest.

Sometimes these interests are lifelong; in other cases, they change at unpredictable intervals. In either case, most people with Asperger's syndrome have one or two intense interests at any given time. In pursuit of these interests, the person with Asperger's often manifests extremely sophisticated reason, an almost obsessive focus, and an enormous capacity to memorize facts.

Children and adolescents with Asperger's syndrome often have little patience for things that lie outside their areas of interest. At school, they are often unmotivated to do regular homework assignments; others, however, may be obsessively motivated to outperform their school peers. Sometimes, the combination of social problems and intense interests can lead to unusual behavior, such as greeting a stranger by launching into a lengthy discussion of a special interest.

Speech and Language Peculiarities

People with Asperger's syndrome often speak in a very formal, structured way. A five-year-old child with this condition, for example, might speak in language that could easily have come from a university textbook, especially on his or her special area of interest.

Literal interpretation is another common characteristic of this condition. For instance, one researcher gives the example of a girl with Asperger's syndrome who was asked on the phone, "Is Paul there?" Although Paul was in the house, he was not in the room with her, so she simply said "no" and hung up. The person on the other end had to call back and explain that he meant for her to find Paul and bring him to the telephone.

Many people with Asperger's syndrome also use words in unique ways, coining new usages and putting strange combinations of words together. They also may enjoy word games, including puns and rhymes. Their verbal skills may even fall in the genius range in some cases.

Other Characteristics

Those affected by Asperger's may also experience a range of other perception and developmental *anomalies*. Children with Asperger's, for example, may be slow to develop *fine motor skills*. Others may have an odd way of walking or display compulsive finger, hand, or arm movements. In general, people with Asperger's like things to be neat and orderly. They usually like to stick to a predictable schedule; if the same thing does not happen at the same time every day, they may become anxious.

Some people with Asperger's are extremely sensitive to sensory experiences; too many smells, sounds, tastes, sights, and **tactile** sensations can

One of the common symptoms of Asperger's involves an intense focus on topics such as dinosaurs.

make them feel overwhelmed. Often, they prefer soft clothing and familiar tastes and scents. Some may even become extremely upset by loud noises or strong smells, or they may dislike being touched. This condition, often referred to as sensory overload, may make school more difficult for these children, where being jostled by other kids and the levels of noise in the classroom can become intolerable for them. Some of these children may also be unable to block out certain repetitive sensory stimuli, such as the constant ticking of a clock. Whereas most children stop registering this sound after a short time, if the sound is not removed, a child with Asperger's can become distracted, upset, or even (in rare cases) violent.

People with Asperger's syndrome are also more prone to psychiatric disorders, including depression, *oppositional defiant disorder*, *attention-deficit hyperactivity disorder (ADHD)*, anxiety, *obsessive-compulsive disorder*, and *bipolar disorder*.

The Latest Research: Boys vs. Girls

One way researchers define the characteristics of autism spectrum disorders (including Asperger's syndrome) is a deficit in Theory of Mind (ToM)—the ability of a child to understand that others have beliefs, desires, and intentions that are different from his own.

Building on and extending research on ToM, researchers from the Cambridge University's department of experimental psychology, Lawson,

Some children with Asperger's may feel overwhelmed by loud noises or large crowds. This can make school even more challenging.

People with Asperger's are more likely to have psychiatric disorders such as depression.

Baron-Cohen, and colleagues, proposed that ToM is based on two psychological dimensions: empathizing and systematizing. These researchers defined empathizing as the drive to identify emotions and thoughts of others—and then to respond emotionally in an appropriate manner. Systemizing they defined as the drive to analyze and build systems such as those used in machines, mathematics, and technical techniques.

Researchers already knew that males are much better at systematizing compared to empathizing, while females excel in empathizing. This suggested to the Cambridge psychologists the possibility that autism and Asperger's syndrome is an extreme version of the normal male pattern of ToM.

To test this model, Lawson and his colleagues compared eighteen males with Asperger's syndrome, forty-four males without Asperger's syndrome, and forty-five typically developing females from the general population in two multiple-choice tests. The first measured empathizing, using the Social Stories Questionnaire (SSQ), which contains ten short stories involving blatant or subtle remarks made by one character that could upset another character in the story. The second test used by the researchers, related to systematizing, was the Physical Prediction Questionnaire (PPQ), which involves understanding physical systems; it was designed to be challenging enough so as to reveal individual differences.

For the SSQ empathizing test, females scored significantly higher than males without Asperger's syndrome, who in turn scored higher than males with

Asperger's. Conversely, on the PPQ systematizing task, females scored significantly lower than both male groups—who did not differ significantly from each other.

What conclusions did the researchers reach? First, on average, males have better systematizing skills than females, females have better empathizing skills, and males with Asperger's syndrome have an extreme form of these two skills with lower empathizing and superior systematizing. The researchers concluded

Psychologists at Cambridge University did a study that found that females are more interested than males in identifying the emotions and thoughts of others.

that more studies are needed to confirm these results.

And why is this important? Because the more we can understand Asperger's syndrome, the better we can help young people with Asperger's cope with their unique characteristics. What's more, understanding the neurological causes of Asperger's syndrome can help teachers, family, and friends be more tolerant of the idiosyncrasies these young people demonstrate.

Chapter 3
Dreams and Nightmares

Wednesday was Duncan's least favorite day. Every Wednesday, he would wake up an hour and a half early, and his brother would drive him fifteen minutes into town, where he attended a small meeting in a room above the YMCA. The room had a circle of chairs, all facing one another, and a water cooler with two neat stacks of paper cups beside it. Wednesday was social-skills training day.

Duncan had been attending these meetings since fifth grade, but he still never felt comfortable. He just didn't quite fit in—not even among a group of kids with all sorts of pervasive developmental disorders, also known as the autism spectrum. At first, Duncan had recoiled from the idea of being associated with a group that included all sorts of autistics. Duncan considered himself to be extremely intelligent and well functioning in many ways—and he certainly was. He refused to consider the idea that he might benefit from the exercises, despite his instructors' insistence they might help him.

Eventually, his embarrassment wore away, and Duncan protested less to the meetings, but he rarely joined in. His embarrassment was replaced by a sense of stubborn indifference. Duncan considered all the exercises taught during the Wednesday morning class to be useless to him. Today, with his audition for the lead role in *Jazz Like That* only hours away, Duncan found himself more anxious to leave the meeting than ever before.

When Sarah had asked him to think about auditioning last week, two of Duncan's worlds had collided at once: his love of music and his love of Sarah. He could hear the notes perfectly in his head, repeating themselves over and over again. In Duncan's mind, everything hung on his performing well at today's audition: not just his hopes for music, but also his hopes for Sarah.

School was a blur once he got there; it didn't seem to happen at all. Duncan's classes seemed more like background imagery, a montage of images beneath his audition song. He was auditioning for the part of Leo—the introspective, quiet, handsome, and insanely wealthy son of an oppressive oil baron. The part required a tenor voice, as well as considerable experience singing jazz.

Duncan hadn't sung in public since he'd been diagnosed with Asperger's, and now he paced outside the auditorium's double-doors, waiting for the girl to open them and read his name off her clipboard. Finally, the moment arrived. "Duncan Watson?"

"I'm here!" Duncan practically shouted.

"Hi. Please come in."

When the door shut behind him, and his eyes adjusted to the dark, cool auditorium, Duncan realized this was a place he wanted to be. The stage was exactly how he imagined it: black, except for a warm pool of white light centered in front of a grand piano. He shuffled quickly down the center aisle toward the stage, glancing briefly at three adults seated in the middle of the auditorium, all of whom he recognized. Mr. Harmon, the director, flashed a brief smile of encouragement at him, but Duncan didn't bother to smile back. That was something he mostly forgot to do, although he knew he was supposed to—and now, he was simply too excited to think of it.

On stage, Duncan handed his music to the pianist, who nodded approvingly of his choice, and said, "Ah, yes. This is my favorite of Leo's solos. Excellent choice." The pianist smiled, but again, Duncan forgot to respond. His face was blank as his eyes scanned the stage, sizing it up, making sure nothing here would disrupt the routine he had prepared when rehearsing his song. Everything had to be just as he had rehearsed.

"Thanks so much for coming out today, Duncan," said a voice from the darkness of the auditorium. "I'm Mr. Har—"

"I know who you are," Duncan interrupted.

"Oh. Well then. This is Mrs. Stewart, our musical director, and this is Mr. Kent, our choreographer."

Duncan was unaware he'd been rude. "I know them too."

"Ah, I see." said Mr. Harmon, "Well then I suppose it's time for us to meet you. You can begin whenever you're ready, Duncan."

Duncan looked quickly to the pianist, and said, "Begin on the count of three." He paused only a moment. "One, two, three."

Almost immediately, Duncan knew something was wrong. The tempo was entirely too quick. The piece was clearly marked at 120 beats per minute, and Duncan surmised the pianist was playing it at 130, maybe 135. With the first verse rapidly approaching, Duncan panicked; any sense of repetition or ritual had forsaken him with this strange new tempo.

"Stop, stop, stop!" he shouted. "You're playing it at least ten beats too fast. It's 120, just like the page says."

The room fell terribly silent.

"Can we try it again at 120?" he asked again.

Still, there was silence. Finally, the pianist said, "I think we can do that." She sounded more startled than upset, and she flipped back the page and began again, this time at the correct tempo.

But the damage had already been done. Duncan's confidence was gone. The next four minutes of singing went by in a scattered flurry. After he finished the song, he didn't even stop to ask for his sheet music back. He immediately began walking up the auditorium toward the double-doors, unsure if he had even sung the song at all. It all seemed so surreal. *I've failed* he thought. *I've completely crushed any chance I had.* As he rushed through the double-doors, he barely heard Mr. Harmon call out, "We'll have parts posted on my office door tomorrow morning!"

Duncan didn't sleep much that night. The hours he did sleep were filled with horrible dreams. In one dream, Duncan watched Sarah crossing a street. She couldn't see a fast-moving car coming from her left, and Duncan tried to call out and warn her, but his voice wouldn't work. He kicked, jumped, and strained until his throat hurt, but he couldn't make a sound. The hood of the car slammed into Sarah's legs just as Duncan's alarm went off, jarring him awake with a gasp. He looked at the glaring red numbers of his clock with despair. *Why get up?* he thought. *I've got no reason to be awake today except to stay away from more bad dreams.*

At his locker, before first period began, Duncan overheard Lacey talking to one of Sarah's other friends, Michelle. "Yeah, she didn't get a lead, but she definitely got a part. She's a minor character—Tess, I think. All I know is she has to kiss some weirdo I've never heard of."

Well at least Sarah got a part, Duncan thought, closing his locker and heading to class. He had walked half way to physics when he stopped in the middle of the hallway and dropped his books. *Wait a minute—Sarah got the part of Tess. And Tess has to kiss Leo. And Leo is played by some weirdo, and I'M some weirdo!*

Duncan scooped up his books and dashed toward Mr. Harmon's office.

When he arrived, Sarah and a group of theater kids were gathered around the small piece of loose-leaf paper taped to the door. They were all pushing and pointing, laughing and talking about their parts. Duncan couldn't see the list from where he was standing, and no one seemed to notice him on the outside of the group. He stood on his toes, but he couldn't make out the small handwriting from that distance. And then Sarah's voice rose above the chatter: "Hey, everybody, look at this, Leo finally decided to show up."

She was smiling and pointing to Duncan.

Who "Discovered" Asperger's Syndrome?

In the 1940s, Hans Asperger in Austria identified a unique group of children. These children possessed normal or above-average intelligence, but they had difficulty relating to other people in normal ways.

Twenty years later, Dr. Lorna Wing, an English psychiatrist and physician, became interested in autism as a result of her daughter showing these symptoms. In 1981, she wrote an academic paper that popularized the research of Hans Asperger and coined the term "Asperger's syndrome." Until the

Though Asperger's was first described in the 1940s, it was not officially defined until 1994.

publication of the fourth edition of the American Psychiatric Association's *Diagnostic and Statistical Manual* (DSM-IV) in 1994, however, there was no officially agreed-upon definition of Asperger's syndrome.

How Is Asperger's Syndrome Diagnosed?

Currently, there are no blood tests or brain scans that can be used to diagnose Asperger's syndrome. Although most children with Asperger's syndrome

Unfortunately, there are no simple blood tests that can be used to diagnose Asperger's syndrome.

are diagnosed between five and nine years of age, many are not diagnosed until they become adults, and misdiagnoses are common. Asperger's syndrome has been confused with other neurological disorders, such as **Tourette's syndrome**, ADHD, oppositional defiant disorder, and obsessive-compulsive disorder (OCD). Some researchers think that Asperger's syndrome may overlap with some types of learning disabilities.

Diagnostic Criteria

In 1994, when Asperger's syndrome first appeared as a separate diagnostic category in the DSM-IV, its definition was justified on the basis of a large international *field trial* of over a thousand children and adolescents. The DSM-IV-TR specified the following diagnostic *criteria* for Asperger's syndrome:

- The child's social interactions are impaired in at least two of the following ways: markedly limited use of nonverbal communication (facial expressions, for example); lack of age-appropriate peer relationships; failure to share enjoyment, interests, or accomplishments with others; lack of reciprocity (turn-taking) in social interactions.

- The child's behavior, interests, and activities are characterized by repetitive or rigid patterns, such as an abnormal preoccupation with one or two topics, or with parts of objects; repetitive physical movements; or rigid insistence on certain routines and rituals.

- The patient's social, occupational, or educational functioning is significantly impaired.
- The child has normal age-appropriate language skills.
- The child has normal age-appropriate cognitive skills, self-help abilities, and curiosity about the environment.
- The child does not meet criteria for another specific PDD or schizophrenia.

To establish the diagnosis, a child psychiatrist or psychologist observes the child and interviews parents and teachers. She also gathers a comprehensive medical and social history.

The diagnostic criteria of the DSM-IV have been criticized for being vague and *subjective*: a condition that one psychologist might define as a "significant impairment" might be viewed differently by another psychologist.

The diagnosis of Asperger's syndrome is also complicated by confusion with other diagnostic categories, such as "high-functioning (IQ higher than 70) autism" (also called HFA) and "schizoid personality disorder of childhood." Unlike schizoid personality disorder of childhood, however, Asperger's syndrome is not an unchanging set of personality traits; symptoms can differ at different ages in the individual's life. Asperger's syndrome can also be distinguished from HFA by the following characteristics:

- later onset of symptoms (usually around three years of age)

Limited use of facial expression is one of the criteria used to diagnose Asperger's syndrome.

- early development of grammatical speech; the Asperger's syndrome child's verbal IQ (scores on verbal sections of standardized intelligence tests) is usually higher than performance IQ (how well the child performs in school). The reverse is usually true for autistic children.

- less severe deficiencies in social and communication skills

Asperger's syndrome is not a static set of personality traits. Symptoms can differ at different ages.

- presence of intense interest in one or two topics
- physical clumsiness and lack of coordination
- family is more likely to have a history of the disorder
- lower frequency of neurological disorders
- more positive outcome in later life

In *A Guide to Asperger Syndrome* (Cambridge University Press, 2002), Christopher Gillberg criticizes the "no significant delay" described by the DSM-IV as being an oversimplification of the syndrome. He states that although there may well be significant delay in some areas of language development, it is often combined with exceptionally high functioning in other language-related areas. He argues that this combination is very different from normal language development.

Because of criticisms like this, clinicians sometimes use slightly different sets of diagnostic criteria besides the DSM-IV definition. Other instruments that have been used to identify children with Asperger's syndrome include Gillberg's criteria, a six-item list compiled by a Swedish researcher that specifies problems in social interaction, a preoccupying narrow interest, forcing routines and interests on the self or others, speech and language problems, nonverbal communication problems, and physical clumsiness; and the Australian Scale for Asperger's Syndrome, a detailed multi-item questionnaire developed in 1996.

...TIONNAIRE

...y often ☐

...ften ☐

...Sometimes ☐

☑

Rarely

Other instruments used to diagnose Asperger's include a six-item list called Gillberg's criteria and a multi-item questionnaire known as the Australian Scale for Asperger's Syndrome.

Brain Imaging

Current research has connected Asperger's syndrome with only a few structural abnormalities of the brain. Findings include abnormally large folds in the brain tissue in the left frontal region, abnormally small folds in the operculum (a lid-like structure composed of portions of three adjoining brain lobes), and damage to the left temporal lobe (a part of the brain containing a sensory area associated with hearing). The first single photon emission tomography (SPECT) study of a person with Asperger's syndrome found a lower-than-normal supply of blood to the left parietal area of the brain, an area associated with body sensations. Brain imaging studies on a larger sample of people with AS are ongoing.

The Latest Research: Seeking Earlier Diagnoses

Children with autism are usually first diagnosed because of their failure to develop language skills. This means they are diagnosed fairly early, usually before they are three years old. Children with Asperger's syndrome, however, are not generally diagnosed until several years later, when they are around six or seven years old. Because their symptoms are not as severe, they often escape notice for several years.

Researchers are seeking ways to counteract this issue by identifying Asperger's traits that can be recognized earlier in a child's development. Members of the psychology department at the University of Florida, for example, have suggested infants' movement patterns can be thought of as their "first language"—and may be a more accurate way of identifying Asperger's early in a child's life, since the development of motor skills is a baby's central task in the first year of life.

The researchers used the Eshkol-Wachman movement notation (EWMN), a movement analysis designed to enable dance *choreographers* to write movement down on paper, which dancers can later reconstruct in its entirety (similar to a musical score). The EWMN is a very detailed analysis of a person's movement.

The researchers at the University of Florida used this method to analyze videotapes of sixteen infants who had already been diagnosed with Asperger's syndrome. The detailed analysis looked at infants' mouth movements, as well as their patterns of lying down, standing up, sitting or crawling, falling down, and movement while being tilted. Many movement deficits were seen in the infants studied. For example, the infants in the study had an abnormally shaped mouth during smiling; their neck reflexes when righting themselves from a lying-down to prone position were either abnormal or *asymmetrical*; they frequently failed to adjust a normal shift of weight and fell down frequently; when they fell, they didn't use protective reflexes to catch themselves; and they failed to keep their heads oriented properly when they were tilted. Normal infants showed none of these deficits.

Since a baby's reflexes and movements are easy to spot, they can be used as early detection signs. When these reflexes persist too long or do not appear when they should, the motor development of the infant— and subsequently, other aspects of his behavior—will be affected. These movement reflexes can therefore serve as early detection markers for abnormal neurological development in Asperger's syndrome.

Why is this important? Because if a child's condition is not identified until she is seven years old, she has already missed out on several years of treatment.

Chapter 4
Risks

Duncan never knew that someone's hand could fit so perfectly into his own. He still didn't understand why Sarah seemed to like him, but he was too happy to ask many questions. Since rehearsals had begun, Duncan needed Sarah more than ever. She was a spokesperson for him when he couldn't defend himself or was misrepresented.

In school, word had gotten out that Duncan Watson, the kid who punched Mr. Thomas in fourth grade, would play the lead role in the fall musical. Many kids found the idea of Duncan as an actor—let alone a lead actor—very funny. For a brief period in middle school, many of the kids had called Duncan "slate face" because his facial expressions were so blank. When they did occur, his expressions were often peculiar or inappropriate to the situation. The thought of him trying to act seemed pretty silly.

In fact, Mr. Harmon had been working on this very issue with Duncan during rehearsals. Then one day after rehearsal, Duncan had approached Mr. Harmon in tears. He had watched video footage of himself rehearsing on stage, and he'd seen how limited his use of gesture was; how clumsy his body language; how difficult it was for him to adjust his physical proximity to other actors; and, of course, how stiff and peculiar his gaze often seemed. But Mr. Harmon dismissed all these things as secondary. He encouraged Duncan to consider the true spirit of an actor: one who takes action.

Through his conversations with Mr. Harmon, Duncan discovered much about acting, but much more about living in general. Mr. Harmon said that good acting required a clear objective, and strong choices to achieve that objective. This was a concept that Duncan could apply to his struggle with Asperger's syndrome. It allowed Duncan to acknowledge his limited abilities, while it also affirmed his power to make strong choices. He could choose to hide from the strange, often harsh world, or he could choose to engage with it, perhaps even learn from it.

Of course, Sarah was very important in convincing Duncan that time spent learning to cope with AS was time well spent. She and Duncan now sat beside one another in the front row of physics class. She was never far from his side, especially after rehearsals, when she would encourage him to hang around and make small talk with the rest of the cast. Those five to ten minutes of small talk were very difficult for Duncan. He felt undeserving of his lead role, and he wondered if this close group of friends resented him. They never seemed to, though; he'd never been around a group of people before who seemed so unfazed by his often strange, sometimes lengthy remarks. These people didn't run away from him.

As Duncan confronted people more frequently, more conflicts found their way into his life. Fortunately, Mr. Harmon had taken a liking to Duncan—both for his talent as a singer and for his heart to learn—and he had become an advocate for Duncan. Mr. Harmon was the special education teacher at Washington Senior High, and he invited Duncan to his office as a place of solace, should he need one at any point during the day. Mr. Harmon also encouraged each of Duncan's teachers to do their own research on Asperger's syndrome. Most teachers had only what little information was provided to them by the school, and Mr. Harmon could see that what Duncan needed most was an environment where he could take risks and make strong choices. The public school system provided very few resources to make that possible, but Mr. Harmon was doing his best to create a niche for Duncan where he could safely explore his risks and choices.

Duncan's parents were worried about their son's recent choices, however. They knew he was spending a great deal of time with a girl named Sarah, and they also knew he had a lead in the musical. They were concerned Duncan was taking on too much, too quickly. They still remembered the days of elementary school and early middle school, days when they would wince every time the phone rang, expecting the daily phone call reporting on Duncan's troublemaking. Their experience had taught them that their son didn't handle pressure well; they weren't sure they wanted him to take any risks, not if they could lead to him losing his temper and getting in trouble.

But Duncan forged ahead, despite his parents' fears. He did, of course, encounter many bumps. But nothing seemed insurmountable. Especially, when he had Sarah's support.

The final week of dress rehearsals had arrived, and by now, Duncan wasn't the only one feeling stressed. After all, they had a show to perform on Friday night, only four days away.

Duncan was backstage in front of a standing mirror, buttoning up Leo's dinner vest, when Ashley, one of Sarah's friends in the cast, came around the corner with tears in her eyes. Duncan wasn't sure if she was upset. "Are you sad, Ashley?"

"Oh. Hey, Duncan. I don't know. I feel like I'm going to die."

Duncan thought for a moment about Ashley's words. Ryan and his therapist had often explained to him about "figurative language," about sarcasm, and how people often used both to be funny. Duncan knew that Ashley didn't mean she was actually going to die, so he figured she must be joking. Trying hard to be polite—because he really liked Ashley—he let out a loud belt of laughter. "Good one, Ashley!"

Ashley stared at him, then started crying harder than before. She left the dressing room with her hands over her eyes. Duncan looked after her, unsure what to do. Should he follow her and apologize? Or was she still joking?

He heard Mr. Harmon call out, "One minute until places, please!" so Duncan kept buttoning his vest.

A few moments later, Sarah entered the room looking angry. "I can't believe you, Duncan. Ashley was having a terrible day already. That wasn't necessary."

He tried to respond but she had turned and left already.

"Everyone get in place!" Mr. Harmon called from the back of the auditorium.

That night's rehearsal was one of Duncan's worst, and the next three nights weren't much better. Everyone was worried about him. Sarah approached him after rehearsal on Wednesday night and tried to apologize, but Duncan wouldn't let her. He didn't understand that he should have met her half way; after all, he considered the fault all his own, so why should he listen to her apology?

He spent that whole week preparing a date for him and Sarah on Thursday, after rehearsal. Of course, he should have been preparing for opening night on Friday.

Meanwhile, Sarah was convinced this date was more an imposition than an invitation. She watched as Duncan went through all the motions, checking off boxes on his dating spreadsheet. He gave her flowers; he asked her questions he thought she wanted to be asked; he tried to listen more, and stay away from talking at length about his areas of special interest. In Sarah's eyes, the date was a disaster the moment it began, but in Duncan's, it looked as if he was doing all the right things—so how could anything go wrong? He was blind to Sarah's discomfort.

About thirty minutes into their walk around the park, Sarah stopped and faced Duncan. "Duncan, look: I know you have Asperger's syndrome. I talked to Mr. Harmon about it. Of course, I haven't told anyone else. But I don't understand why you didn't tell me, and why you don't tell more people. It could only help people understand you. You've got to trust some people, eventually."

"And how would you know, Sarah?" Duncan blurted out, embarrassed and a little angry. This conversation wasn't anywhere on his spreadsheet.

She stood there in silence, before saying, "I like you Duncan; I really do. But I'm not sure if you're seeing the real me. I'm not sure if you ever will, because you never even look at me. I'm right here, Duncan. Look at me."

But Duncan couldn't look at her. He never made eye contact with anyone, not if he could help it.

Sarah walked away.

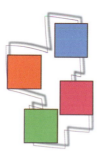

Who Gets Asperger's Syndrome?

Although the incidence of Asperger's syndrome has been variously estimated between 0.024 percent and 0.36 percent of the general population in North America and northern Europe, further research is required to determine its true rate of occurrence, especially since the diagnostic criteria have been defined so recently. In addition, no research regarding the incidence of Asperger's syndrome has been done on the populations of developing countries, and nothing is known about the incidence of the disorder in different racial or ethnic groups. In 1993, a study of the total population of Sweden found that, at a minimum, 3.6 per 1,000 school-aged children definitely meet the criteria for Asperger syndrome. If merely suspected cases are included, the prevalence becomes approximately 7.1 per 1,000. Data for the adult population is not available.

We do know, though, that Asperger's syndrome appears to be much more common in boys. Dr. Asperger's first patients were all boys, but girls have been diagnosed with Asperger's syndrome since the 1980s. One Swedish study found the male-to-female ratio to be four to one; however, the World Health Organization gives the male-to-female ratio as eight to one. Many experts, however, believe that these statistics may not reflect the actual incidence among females, since because little girls are socialized differently from little boys, females with autism with Asperger's may learn to better compensate for their impairments.

Asperger's syndrome seems to be more common in boys than in girls. However, there is no agreement on the male to female ratio.

Asperger's affects both children and adults. However, there is more research about the syndrome in children.

Most of the research on Asperger's syndrome relates to children, while there is more conjecture than hard evidence on how it affects adults. Most people with Asperger's syndrome probably learn to cope with their social impairments later in life. However, there is no "cure" as such. Some adults with this disorder have serious difficulties with social and occupational functioning, while others are able to finish their schooling, join the workforce, and marry and have families.

What Causes Asperger's Syndrome?

Asperger's syndrome appears to run in families, particularly in families with histories of depression and bipolar disorder. Hans Asperger noted that his initial group of patients all had fathers with Asperger's symptoms. Knowledge of the genetic profile of the disorder is limited, however.

About 50 percent of people with AS have a history of oxygen deprivation during the birth process, which has led to the **hypothesis** that the disorder is caused by damage to brain tissue before or during childbirth. Another cause that has been suggested is an organic defect in the functioning of the brain. Research studies have made no connection whatsoever between Asperger's and childhood trauma, abuse, or neglect.

How Is Asperger's Syndrome Treated?

Asperger's syndrome cannot be cured; it is a lifelong condition. However, individuals can learn ways of coping better with their condition. Because each individual is different, however, there is no single treatment *regimen* for all people with AS. Specific treatments are based on the individual's symptom pattern.

The treatment team needed for a child with Asperger's syndrome will vary based on the specifics and the severity of the child's disabilities. Pediatricians, developmental pediatricians, *neurologists*, and child psychiatrists can all play a part in shaping the treatment plan for a child with Asperger's syndrome. Physical therapy, *occupational therapy*, speech and

Because Asperger's tends to run in families, there is thought to be some genetic component to the syndrome.

language therapy, individual and group behavioral therapy, and *psychoeducational* planning are all vital aspects of helping a child with Asperger's syndrome.

Medication

Many children with Asperger's syndrome do not require any medication. For those who do, the drugs that are recommended most often include *psychostimulants* or one of the tricyclic antidepressants (TCAs) for hyperactivity or inattention; beta blockers, neuroleptics (antipsychotic medications), or lithium for anger or aggression; selective serotonin reuptake inhibitors (SSRIs) or TCAs for diminishing rituals (repetitive behaviors) and preoccupations; and SSRIs or TCAs for anxiety symptoms. St. John's wort, an herbal remedy, has been tried with some success with Asperger's syndrome patients.

Psychotherapy

Although Asperger's syndrome is not caused by emotional trauma, patients often benefit from individual psychotherapy, particularly during adolescence. Talking with a counselor can help these individuals cope with depression and other painful feelings related to their social difficulties. Many children with Asperger's syndrome are also helped by group therapy, which brings them together with others facing the same challenges. As they recognize that there are other people who are like them, they feel less isolated and lonely; they are more able to recognize that they have a specific physical condition that makes them different but not "bad."

Medication is not required for many children with Asperger's. Those children that do take medication are most likely to take psychostimulants or tricyclic antidepressants.

Behavioral approaches also work well with these children. Play therapy can be helpful in teaching the child to recognize social cues, while adults with Asperger's syndrome are most likely to benefit from individual therapy using a *cognitive-behavioral* approach; many also attend group therapy. Some adults have been helped with their language skills by working with speech therapists. A relatively new approach called behavioral coaching has been used to help adults with Asperger's learn to organize and set priorities for their daily activities.

The Latest Research: Drug Treatment and Asperger's Syndrome

Traditionally, drug treatment is not prescribed for people with Asperger's syndrome. But new research studies are investigating whether these individuals might benefit from drug treatments after all.

Asperger's Syndrome and Antipsychotic Medications

Researchers already knew that the newer types of antipsychotic medications, which block brain receptors for the *neurotransmitters* dopamine and serotonin, are effective for treating adults with schizophrenia. Now, in a study reported in the *New England Journal of Medicine*, scientists are investigating whether these same medications may be beneficial to children with Asperger's syndrome and other forms of autism. The investigators compared the usage of risperidone, an antipsychotic drug, with a **placebo** in the treatment of children with an autism disorder accompanied by severe tantrums, aggression, or self-injurious behavior.

The trial was double blind; in other words, the children, their parents, and their doctors did not know whether the children were receiving an active drug or placebo. A total of 101 children (eighty-two boys and nineteen girls, with a mean age, 8.8 years) were randomly assigned to receive risperidone (forty-nine children) or the placebo (fifty-two children). The primary outcome measures were the score on

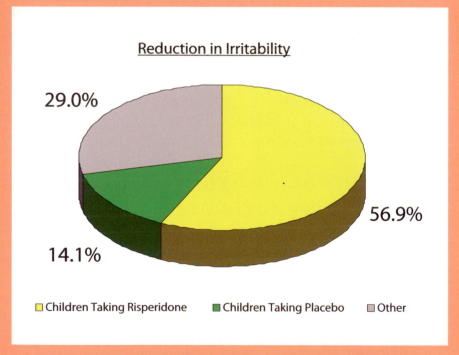

New research is showing that risperidone, an antipsychotic drug, reduces irritability and aggression in children with Asperger's and autism.

the Irritability subscale of the Aberrant Behavior Checklist and the rating on the Clinical Global Impressions Improvement (CGI-I) scale at eight weeks after treatment.

Treatment with risperidone for eight weeks (with a dose range of 0.5 to 3.5 mg per day) resulted in a 56.9 percent reduction in the Irritability score, compared with a 14.1 percent score decrease in the placebo group. In two-thirds of the children with a positive response to risperidone at eight weeks, the benefit was maintained at six months.

The study indicated that risperidone was effective for the treatment of tantrums, aggression, or self-injurious behavior in children with some form of autistic disorder. Despite this significant result, the authors caution: "Nonetheless, the adverse events observed in our study and the lack of a clear benefit with regard to core symptoms of autism indicate that risperidone should be reserved for treatment of moderate-to-severe behavioral problems associated with autism."

SSRIs and Pervasive Developmental Disorders

A class of drugs called selective serotonin reuptake inhibitors (SSRIs), traditionally prescribed for depression, have also been shown to significantly improve symptoms associated with pervasive developmental disorders (PDDs) such as autism and Asperger's syndrome. At the University of Connecticut School of Medicine, Dr. Namerow and her colleagues studied the medical charts of fifteen children and adolescents with Asperger syndrome, autism, or PDD not otherwise specified between the ages of six and sixteen, who were treated with citalopram, a new SSRI drug. All individuals were clinically diagnosed with PDDs, and were at least moderately to severely impaired by their symptoms. The investigators rated improvement in PDD symptoms before drug (baseline) and at last visit using the CGI Severity and Improvement scale.

Eleven adolescents (73 percent) showed significant improvement in PDD symptoms, anxiety, or mood. Anxiety associated with PDDs improved significantly in 66 percent of patients, and mood improved significantly in 47 percent of patients. Five patients (33 percent) reported mild side effects such as headache, sedation, or agitation, none of which were severe enough to require that the children be removed from the medication.

Oxytocin, Vasopressin, and Asperger's Repetitive Motions

Children with Asperger's syndrome frequently demonstrate repetitive behaviors that include **compulsive** behaviors, unusual attachments to objects, rigid adherence to routines or rituals, and repetitive mannerisms such as self-stimulation. Their social deficits include lack of eye contact, reduced ability to carry on a conversation, and reduced interaction skills. Research done at Mount Sinai School of Medicine suggests that certain protein substances normally found in the brain—oxytocin and vasopressin—may contribute to both repetitive behaviors and social deficits in children with Asperger's syndrome. Further research evidence supporting this theory has shown that the nervous system pathways that control the normal release of these substances are abnormal in individuals with autism and Asperger's disorder.

While oxytocin is known to cause uterine contractions during labor, recent research suggests that oxytocin and vasopressin also play a role in developing normal cognition and social behavior. These two proteins also have been linked to social learning and behavior in rats and monkeys.

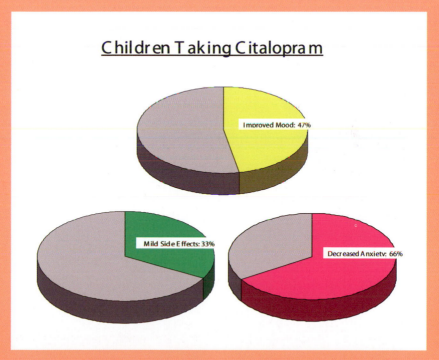

Children Taking Citalopram

Improved Mood: 47%

Mild Side Effects: 33%

Decreased Anxiety: 66%

A study at the University of Connecticut found that adolescents with Asperger's syndrome, who were given citalopram, showed improvement in symptoms while under treatment.

Particularly, oxytocin is important in the retention of newly formed memories and is critical for learning associations, such as the smells of things.

The investigators at Mount Sinai examined the effects of oxytocin on repetitive behaviors in fifteen young adults with autism or Asperger's disorder. Each patient received via an **IV** oxytocin or placebo on separate visits every two to three weeks to determine the effect of the drug; the study was double blind (neither the patient nor the doctor knew whether the active oxytocin agent or a placebo was being given). The researchers measured six repetitive behaviors in the patients: the need to know, repeating, ordering,

Children with Asperger's often have abnormal sleep patterns. Inadequate sleep may cause other symptoms of Asperger's to worsen.

need to tell/ask, self-injury, and touching. Patients with some form of autistic disorders showed a significant reduction in repetitive behaviors after infusion with oxytocin as compared with placebo infusion.

Asperger's Syndrome and Sleep

As many as 65 percent of children with autistic disorder have abnormal sleep patterns, and sleep disturbances are even more common in individuals with Asperger's disorder. Adequate sleep is particularly important in these individuals because sleep disturbances may worsen other symptoms. Researchers at the University of Helsinki, Finland, Dr. Paavonen and her colleagues, studied the effectiveness of the hormone melatonin in treating sleep disturbances in children with Asperger's disorder. Melatonin is a hormone naturally secreted by the body's pineal gland, which functions to initiate sleep, and has been used in the past to promote sleep in various sleep disturbances.

For this study, the researchers studied both sleep characteristics as well as daytime behavior of fifteen children and adolescents (thirteen boys, two girls) with Asperger's syndrome between the ages of six and seventeen. Subjects were given melatonin pills (3 mg/day) for fourteen days. Sleep and daytime behavior were observed 1.5 weeks before, during (at the end of the fourteen days), and three weeks after the treatment period.

Sleep patterns of all children improved during treatment. Time to fall asleep decreased by half (from an average of about forty minutes to twenty-one

Continued research helps to develop new and better treatment methods that will help children with Asperger's lead happy lives.

minutes) in all children. The time they slept (about eight hours) did not change with treatment, but decreased significantly after melatonin was stopped. Despite the short period of this study, most behavioral measures improved. Particularly, depression, anxiety, and withdrawal decreased during the period of treatment. Most of the positive effects disappeared three weeks after melatonin was discontinued. Only two children reported mild tiredness and one reported headache while taking melatonin, but these symptoms went away after the child stopped taking melatonin.

This was the first clinical study using melatonin in children with Asperger's syndrome. The results showed that melatonin may be effective in treating sleep problems in children with Asperger's syndrome. The authors concluded that giving melotonin in low doses (such as used in this study) "can improve sleep quality without virtually any adverse effects."

So why are these research studies important? Because studies can show psychiatrists new and more effective ways of helping children with Asperger's live productive and happy lives.

Chapter 5
Learning the Language

Duncan sat in his bedroom behind a closed door, strumming four quiet chords underneath his worried thoughts. Sarah's words were still stinging: *I'm right here, Duncan. Look at me.*

If only he could make her understand. It wasn't his feelings for her that were absent; it was the ability to show those feelings properly. On his bedside table lay a pamphlet on Asperger's that he'd picked up earlier that week at social-training class. The question-and-answer section at the bottom of the first page seemed to mock him:

What is the principal symptom of Asperger's syndrome?

The profound inability to connect to socially normal people.

The principal behavior?

Compulsively focusing on things other than personal rela-
tionships at the expense of personal relationships.

The last sentence continued to glare at him as he considered last night's events. Duncan wished there was a way
to make Sarah understand he was a faulty car—when he
wanted to turn right, his blinkers said left, and when he
wanted to honk the horn and wave at someone passing by,
windshield-wiper fluid shot out, blurring his world. He
wondered if it would always be this way.

He heard a knock on his door and his brother's voice:
"We've got to leave for school in five minutes, bro. Tonight's
a big night for you, I hope you got some sleep."

Duncan barely nodded, and kept on strumming the
same four chords in his head.

Ryan was quiet for a moment, then opened the door,
walked across the room, and sat next to Duncan. He picked
up Duncan's guitar. "I know what this is about, and I have
the solution. It's been helping broken hearts for over a hun-
dred years, and it's called the blues, brother." Ryan started
picking out a few notes on the blues scale, occasionally slap-
ping his pick-hand on his thigh to keep a slow beat. Then
he started singing, a sound that vaguely resembled croak-
ing: "Woman, why you go and do me so wrong?" He missed

three or four strings whenever he sang, and the beat became erratic. "Woman, I used to feel so strong. Now I don't know where I belong."

Duncan couldn't take it any longer. "You sound terrible! You're not helping."

"Well then help me out and sing along, Dunc. I've got the groove goin' for you."

Duncan wasn't amused.

"If you don't want to, I'll keep singing. I can be here all morning." Ryan said.

Duncan stared at his brother, and then, without thinking, he sang: "Bein' different, well it ain't so baaad. Until some pretty lady, go and make you sad."

Ryan hooted his approval and cranked up the tempo on the beat, while Duncan sang the same line over and over again. Ryan was never very good at guitar, and even though he seemed to enjoy the sounds he made (he closed his eyes and kind of hummed a contented "mmhmm" every few minutes), Duncan couldn't take the missed notes anymore; his ears were very sensitive, especially to jarring pitches. He pushed Ryan's hand off the fret board, and they both laughed this time.

"So what did Sarah do?" Ryan asked.

Duncan shrugged. "It's not her fault. That's just the thing. It's all me. It's all me. But there's nothing to do. I can't change; I can't fix myself; I can't make her understand."

"Whoa. Whoa. Slow down. First of all, there's plenty to be done. Second of all, 'fixing you' is not what she wants. She likes you, bro. That's obvious. It can't be that hard to show her you like her. I mean, I'm a geek too, Dunc. I am the Jedi master of awkward romance. But you just make it work. Now come on, let's go to school—we're gonna be late." Ryan stood up, but Duncan stayed seated.

"Listen, Ryan." Duncan said quietly. "Do you have any idea what it's like to never feel safe? To be blind to people's thoughts and words? To live without the language that everyone else is speaking, too slow to learn a few words to impress a girl? I've spent years trying to stay quiet, hoping no one catches on to my secret. I haven't stayed silent because I don't have anything to say; I've stayed silent because I don't know how to say it. When I speak, people just look at me weird—like they're confused, or even scared. Nice people only make it worse—they say hello, grit their teeth to have a conversation with me, smile politely, and walk away. Inside of myself, I'm banging on glass walls, jumping up and down, trying to get their attention. It's like I'm shouting, 'Here I am, this is the real me! Over here!' And then from inside my walls, I watch them walk away."

Ryan sighed and sat down beside Duncan again. "No. I really don't know what that's like, Dunc. I really don't." They sat in silence for a while. "I'm sorry I presumed to know. But you have to remember that I am your brother.

I know so many of your strengths that sometimes I forget your weaknesses. I forget how hard it is for you. I forget you don't have half as much game as I have with the ladies." He nudged Duncan and winked. "You're the president of our high school's Star Trek club, Duncan."

"Yeah, so? You're the treasurer."

Ryan put a hand on Duncan's shoulder. "Find ways that you already know how to communicate—like music. I've seen you play and I've heard you sing; you're incredible. Music is a language in itself. Where words dare not go, music explores boldly."

Duncan made a face at his brother. "Did you just alter the Star Trek motto, 'to boldly go where no man has gone before,' to make music sound adventurous, and make me feel better?"

"Yes, I did. Did it work?"

"No."

"Okay, well . . . let's try something else then. You were right to focus on language. People with AS have a hard choice: to be bilingual or not. Learn to speak the language of the natives—or not. I've had days when I feel like a stranger in a strange world. Honestly. Everyone does, probably. You're not alone, and you're not incapable, even though the journey ahead seems impossible. You have the intelligence and heart to learn the language of this world."

Later that night, Duncan sat crouched behind three sets of stage curtains, mumbling his lines to himself and listening as the auditorium filled with anticipation. He wasn't sure if he'd be able to stand up when Mr. Harmon called for places in five minutes. What if Ryan was wrong? What if he never learned to speak to other people? What if he never was able to make the people he cared about feel his love?

When the lights came up on the first scene, Duncan sang as loudly as he could, remembering everything Harmon had taught him. The night went by in a blur: the costume changes happened rapidly; the dance numbers came and went; intermission seemed to last only a few seconds. All along, the audience cheered and laughed with the cast, breathing new life into everyone's performance, and before he knew it, Duncan was grasping his co-stars' hands, bowing over and over before a full auditorium that had risen to its feet.

Duncan knew he should have been overwhelmed with happiness. This was what he wanted; this was what he had dreamed about as a little kid, singing along to jazz albums in his living room. But Duncan felt as though he were removed from himself; as though now he were behind the glass walls, and his own body was on the other side. He was watching it all happen around him, unable to touch Sarah's face, or go to his brother in the front row and give him a hug.

As the curtains closed on the thundering applause, Duncan felt almost nothing.

After that weekend, Duncan was well known throughout Washington Senior High. People had heard Duncan sing. He couldn't walk down the hall between classes without three or four students approaching him to compliment his performance as Leo. He should have been glowing, but he wasn't. People who didn't know him patted him on the back, sang snatches of Leo's songs to him in the cafeteria, and one girl had actually asked Duncan to marry her in study hall.

Those who did know Duncan were concerned for him.

Whenever Duncan saw Sarah in the hall, she'd wave and smile, and some days he tried to give her a weak wave in return. He even tried to curve his lips in a sickly smile. It was no good. He would never learn the language. He would never figure out a way to show Sarah how he felt about her.

When Ryan drove Duncan home after opening night, he had practically bubbled over with congratulations. "You did it, buddy! You nailed it!"

Duncan only nodded.

And now he felt like giving up. How could he learn a language that was so alien to everything he was?

But the real changes in Duncan's life were happening without him even realizing. After a few weeks, when the glory of *Jazz Like That* had died away, Duncan expected his life would return to normal again: friendless, songless. But it didn't return to normal—not exactly, at least.

True, kids no longer shook his hand in the hallway, and his smallest actions weren't greeted with thundering applause anymore. But something better than applause started happening: a handful of kids from the cast said hi to Duncan every day. Even Ashley smiled and waved when she saw Duncan walking quickly to the special education room with his arms full of books.

One day, Duncan did something he never thought possible. He was walking toward Mr. Harmon's office when Sarah stepped out of a classroom, walking the same direction as Duncan. She didn't see him. *This is it*, Duncan thought. *Every bone in my body hates the idea of an unplanned conversation with her, but I'll never have another chance if I don't do something soon. Why not now?* Duncan increased his pace to catch up with her.

"Hey Sarah." He tapped her on her right shoulder so she looked the wrong way.   "Hey!" She laughed at the trick. "You startled me!"

I startled myself, Duncan thought. He never did surprising things.

"I'm sorry," he said, worried now that he might have offended her.

"It's okay," she said. "I'm sorry too."

"Why? You didn't startle me."

Sarah laughed again. "No. But I've been making things harder for you. I know you have AS. I should have helped you out, instead of getting my feelings hurt because you have a hard time looking at me."

Duncan looked down at his feet. "I like looking at you. I just can't do it when you're looking back."

Then Sarah startled Duncan: she reached out and hugged him. He didn't normally like to be touched very much, but Sarah's arms felt nice around his shoulders. She smelled good, too.

"I'm joining a support group that meets in Syracuse," he blurted. "I thought you should be the first to know. It's a half hour away, but it's worth it. I did some research and found a group of all AS kids who meet once a week. They talk about a lot of issues that surround AS, like depression and loneliness. They also do social-skills training for facial expressions, social cues—jazz like that." He gave her face a quick glance, trying to see if she realized he was telling a joke. "You know—jazz like that," he repeated, emphasizing the last three words.

Sarah laughed. "I heard you the first time."

"Anyway, I think this group would be really good for me."

Sarah smiled and hugged him again. "Duncan, I'm so proud of you."

The support group meetings turned out to be long and hard—but Duncan knew they were helping him become bilingual: slowly and painfully, he was learning to speak the language everyone else did around him. Duncan even felt like he connected to some of the other students; he considered many of them his friends.

The moderator of the group had them focus on all sorts of issues. They began with social reciprocity, which the instructor defined as "the give and take" in a relationship. They gave special attention to recognizing and interpreting various social circumstances. They role-played, watched videos, and—most important—they learned everything together. Lessons were never taught to one student alone, but always in a group setting where Duncan and the others could experience the lesson more fully. The instructor encouraged the kids to find an upperclassman at their school they could trust, someone who might be a mentor to them. Duncan could think of no one better than his older brother Ryan.

The class encouraged Duncan to look to Ryan for advice and guidance in social situations. Ryan, of course, was more than happy to help—and he wasn't the only one. Mr. Harmon was working with Duncan's parents to find him a counselor, someone to talk to during the week, someone who had experience with and compassion for Asperger's syndrome.

He found such a counselor in Mrs. Valerie Brown, an older woman who agreed to meet with Duncan once during the school week, and as many times outside of school as Duncan wanted. It turned out that this was one of the best relationships Duncan could find. His meetings with Mrs. Brown inside and outside school helped his self-esteem and his ambition.

When spring came around, and the leaves began to glow green again, Mr. Harmon announced that auditions would be held for the second musical of the year. Duncan auditioned, and this time he got a smaller role. But he didn't complain. He had a few good friends, and a few good hopes for the future.

And finally, he was learning to speak the same language Sarah did.

What Lies Ahead for a Young Person with Asperger's?

Asperger's syndrome is a lifelong but stable condition. The prognosis for children with Asperger's syndrome is generally good as far as intellectual development is concerned; as a result, most will be able to be employed as adults and be functioning members of society. Adults with Asperger's syndrome, however, appear to be at greater risk of depression than the general population, and they may also have an increased risk of a psychotic episode (a period of time during which they lose touch with reality).

Asperger's syndrome causes the greatest problems in the realm of social interaction. These problems can be severe, especially during childhood and adolescence, when other children may not understand their differences. Children with Asperger's syndrome are often teased and bullied by other children because they do not act or talk like others their age. The child or teen with Asperger's syndrome is often puzzled and confused when he is mistreated, unaware of what he has done "wrong." Many children with Asperger's create imaginary friends to keep them company and counteract their feelings of loneliness. Even as adults, many people with Asperger's report feeling detached and isolated from the world around them.

Children with Asperger's often display advanced abilities in reading, writing, mathematics, music, and art, sometimes even into the "gifted" range. At the same time, however, as part of their lack of understanding of social conventions, they often

An individual with Asperger's can grow up to lead a successful life. However, the social detachment many feel may cause loneliness and depression.

have little respect for authority. They also have very little patience with tasks they consider to be trivial (such as homework assignments). This combination of characteristics often creates problems between these children and teachers who do not understand their condition. Teachers sometimes consider a child with Asperger's as a "problem child" or a "poor performer"; the teacher may also consider the child to be disrespectful or arrogant. Meanwhile, the child feels frustrated and unjustly wronged—and often lacks the ability to express these feelings.

Children with Asperger's do best in structured learning situations in which they learn problem-solving and social skills as well as academic subjects. In some cases, these children have been mistakenly put in special programs either for children with much lower levels of functioning or for children with conduct disorders. Although they frequently need protection from the teasing and bullying of other children, they should not be isolated from their peers. One approach that has been found helpful at the high-school level is to pair a young adolescent with Asperger's syndrome with a slightly older teenager who can serve as a mentor. The older teen can show the ropes to the younger adolescent, cluing him in on slang, dress code, and cliques.

Social difficulties can cause challenges for individuals with Asperger's syndrome—but they do not doom these people to miserable lives. Individuals with this condition have many assets and strengths. Their intense focus often contributes to a high level of ability in their fields of interest. When these

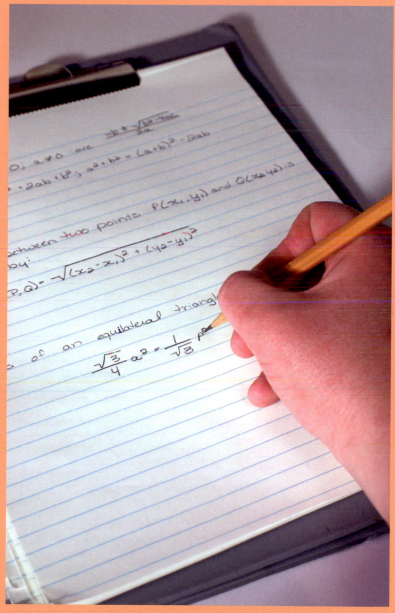

Children with Asperger's are often gifted in subjects like reading, writing, art, music and mathematics.

Students with Asperger's do best in a structured learning environment. They should not be isolated from their peers.

special interests coincide with a materially or socially useful task, the person with Asperger's often can lead a profitable life. For example, the child obsessed with building model boats may grow up to be an accomplished shipwright. Adults with Asperger's syndrome are productively employed in a wide variety of fields. They do best in jobs with regular routines, as well as in occupations that allow them to work in isolation. In large companies, employers and colleagues may need some information about Asperger's syndrome in order to understand the new employee's "eccentricities."

Although many people with Asperger's are not considered socially successful by common standards—and many remain alone their entire lives—some individuals with this condition find understanding people with whom they have close relationships. Many have children.

People with Asperger's syndrome are often very intelligent. Because of their intellectual abilities, they recognize their problem and try to adapt to living among people without the syndrome (even when they are unaware of the term "Asperger's syndrome" or believe it does not apply to them).

As more and more people are diagnosed with Asperger's syndrome, its image has shifted. Many people feel that it should not be considered a disease but a syndrome with both advantages and disadvantages. Prominent people with Asperger's include:

Vernon Smith, Nobel Prize–winning economist
Dan Aykroyd, comedian/actor

Because of their intelligence, people with Asperger's syndrome are able to adapt to living among people without the syndrome.

There is speculation that some famous figures of the past, such as Albert Einstein, might have had Asperger's syndrome.

Gary Numan, industrial rocker
Craig Nicholls, frontman of the band The Vines
Santosh Tajiri, creator of Pokémon

Recently, some researchers have speculated that well-known figures of the past had Asperger's syndrome because they showed some Asperger's-related

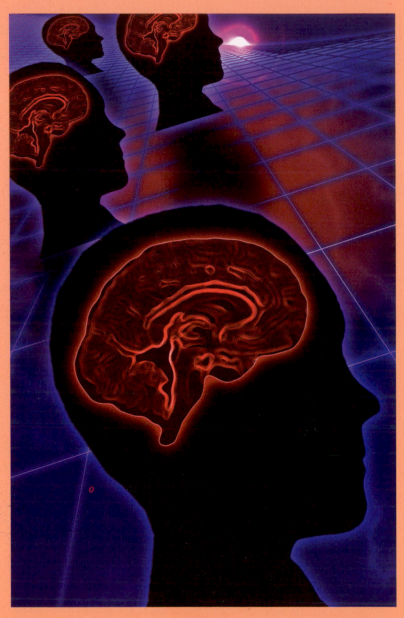

Not everyone's brain works in exactly the same way. This neurodiversity is part of what gives everyone different interests and
abilities.

tendencies or behaviors, such as intense interest in one subject, or social problems. They include:

Isaac Newton, scientist
Albert Einstein, mathematician
Ludwig Wittgenstein, philosopher

Of course, historical figures cannot be accurately diagnosed! But recognizing the contributions of individuals with Asperger-like characteristics helps create role models for children with this syndrome.

An article in *Wired* magazine suggested that Asperger's syndrome is more common among computer technicians. This article created the popular concept that all "geeks" have Asperger's syndrome.

Some people argue with the concept that there is an "ideal" brain and that any deviation from the norm must be considered *pathological*. They demand tolerance for what they call *neurodiversity*.

Our society has little tolerance for people who act differently from everybody else. People with Asperger's syndrome truly march to their own drummers. Their brains function very differently from the average person's, and this causes them to interact with others in unique ways. Clearly, though, these are valuable individuals who have much to offer our world.

Glossary

anomalies: Things that deviate from the norm.

asymmetrical: Not arranged in a balanced manner.

attention-deficit hyperactivity disorder (ADHD): A condition occurring mainly in children, characterized by hyperactivity, inability to concentrate, and impulsive or inappropriate behavior.

atypical: Not conforming to the usual type or expected pattern.

bipolar disorder: A psychiatric condition characterized by extreme highs and extreme lows emotionally, also called manic-depressive disorder.

choreographers: Individuals who plan out dance routines.

chromosome: A rod-shaped structure in the cell nucleus carrying the genes that determine sex and the characteristics an organism inherits from its parents.

cognitive: Relating to the process of acquiring knowledge by the use of reasoning, intuition, or perception.

cognitive-behavioral: Relating to how thoughts influence actions.

compulsive: The need to perform an action repeatedly.

control: A person taking part in an experiment who is not involved in the procedures affecting the rest of the experiment.

criteria: Accepted standards used in making decisions or judgments about something.

empathizing: Identifying with and understanding another person's feelings.

encephalitis: Inflammation of the brain, usually caused by a viral infection.

field trial: A test carried out on a product under conditions of normal use.

fine motor skills: Skills necessary to carry out delicate or intricate tasks.

hypothesis: A tentative explanation for something used as a basis for further investigation.

IV: Intravenous; administered through a vein.

metabolic disorders: Disorders relating to the interrelated series of chemical interactions taking place in living organisms that provide energy and nutrients needed to sustain life.

naive: Having an excessively simple and trusting view of the world and of human nature.

neurodiversity: The belief that atypical neurological wiring is a normal human difference to be accepted and respected as any other human difference.

neurological: Relating to the structure and function of the nervous system.

neurologists: Doctors who specialize in the nervous system.

neurotransmitters: Chemicals that carry messages between neurons.

obsessive-compulsive disorder: A psychiatric disorder characterized by overpowering thoughts to perform a specific action.

occupational therapy: The use of regular periods of suitable productive activity as part of the treatment of illness or a medical condition.

oppositional defiant disorder: An ongoing pattern of uncooperative, defiant, and hostile behavior toward authority figures that interferes with day-to-day functioning.

organic: Characteristic of a living thing.

pathological: Relating to disease.

pervasive: Spreading widely and occupying a great area.

placebo: A substance with no active properties.

psychoeducational: Relating to the underlying mental processes that affect learning.

psychostimulants: Drugs with energizing or mood-elevating effects.

regimen: A prescribed program of medication, diet, exercise, or other measures intended to improve health.

schizophrenia: A psychiatric condition characterized by a loss of contact with reality.

seizures: Convulsions, sensory disturbances, or loss of consciousness resulting from abnormal electrical discharges in the brain (as in epilepsy).

socialization: The action of teaching a person to fit in with society.

spectrum: A range with opposite values at its limits.

stereotypical behaviors: Actions that conform to an oversimplified image or idea held by someone about another group of individuals.

subjective: Based on opinions rather than facts or evidence.

tactile: Relating to the sense of touch.

Tourette's syndrome: A condition in which someone experiences multiple muscular tics and twitches, and utters involuntary vocal grunts and obscene speech.

Further Reading

Bolick, Teresa. *Asperger Syndrome and Adolescence: Helping Preteens & Teens Get Ready for the Real World.* Gloucester, Mass.: Fair Winds Press, 2001.

Haddon, Mark. *The Curious Incident of the Dog in the Night-Time.* New York: Doubleday, 2003.

Jackson, Luke. *Freaks, Geeks and Asperger Syndrome: A User's Guide to Adolescence.* London: Jessica Kingsley, 2000.

Jackson, Luke. *Asperger Syndrome in Adolescence: Living with the Ups, the Downs and Things in Between.* London: Jessica Kingsley, 2003.

Jacobs, Deborah Lynn. *Same Difference.* Unionville, N.Y.: Royal Fireworks Publishing Company, 2000.

Myles, Brenda Smith, and Diane Adreon. *Asperger Syndrome and Adolescence: Practical Solutions for School Success.* Shawnee Mission, Kans.: Autism Asperger Publishing Company, 2001.

Romanowski, Patricia. *The OASIS Guide to Asperger Syndrome: Completely Revised and Updated: Advice, Support, Insight, and Inspiration.* New York: Crown Publishers, 2001.

Sainsbury, Claire. *Martian in the Playground: Understanding the Schoolchild with Asperger's Syndrome.* New York: Lucky Duck Publishing, 2000.

Sanders, Robert S., Jr. *On My Own Terms: My Journey with Asperger's.* Higganum, Conn.: Armstrong Valley Publishing, 2004.

Welton, Jude. *Can I Tell You About Asperger Syndrome?* London: Jessica Kingsley, 2004.

For More Information

ASPEN (Asperger Syndrome Education Network)
www.aspennj.org

Asperger Syndrome
www.autismnsw.com.au

Autism Society of America
www.autism-society.org/site/PageServer

Dallas Asperger Network for Information, Support and Help
www.aspergerinfo.org

Families of Adults Afflicted with Asperger's Syndrome
www.faaas.org

National Organization for Rare Disorders (NORD).
www.rarediseases.org

Online Asperger Syndrome Information and Support
www.aspergersyndrome.org

Weird Not Stupid
www.weirdnotstupid.com

WrongPlanet—International Asperger's Syndrome
Organization
www.wrongplanet.net

Publisher's note:
The Web sites listed on this page were active at the time of publication. The publisher is not responsible for Web sites that have changed their addresses or discontinued operation since the date of publication. The publisher will review and update the Web-site list upon each reprint.

Bibliography

American Psychiatric Association. *Diagnostic and Statistical Manual of Mental Disorders.* 4th edition. Washington, D.C.: American Psychiatric Association, 2000.

Attwood, Antony. *Why Does Chris Do That? Some Suggestions Regarding the Cause and Management of the Children and Adults with Autism and Asperger Syndrome.* Shawnee Mission, Kans.: Autism Asperger Publishing Company, 2003.

Baker, Jed E. *Social Skills Training for Children and Adolescents with Asperger Syndrome and Social-Communications Problems.* Shawnee Mission, Kans.: Autism Asperger Publishing Company, 2003.

Balsamo, Thomas, and Sharon Rosenbloom. *Souls: Beneath and Beyond Autism.* New York: McGraw-Hill, 2003.

Baron-Cohen, Simon. *The Essential Difference: Male and Female Brains and the Truth About Autism*, New York: Basic Books, 2003.

Bolick, Teresa. *Asperger Syndrome and Adolescence: Helping Preteens and Teens Get Ready for the Real World.* Gloucester, Mass.: Fair Winds Press, 2001.

Bruey, Carolyn Thorwarth. *Demystifying Autism Spectrum Disorder: A Guide to Diagnosis for Parents and Professionals.* Bethesda, Md.: Woodbine House, 2004.

Fast, Yvona. *Employment for Individuals With Asperger Syndrome or Non-Verbal Learning Disability: Stories and Strategies.* London: Jessica Kingsley, 2004.

Fitzgerald, Michael. *Autism and Creativity: Is There a Link Between Autism in Men and Exceptional Ability?* New York: Bruner-Routledge, 2004.

Harpur, John, Maria Lawlor, and Michael Fitzgerald. *Succeeding in College with Asperger Syndrome.* London: Jessica Kingsley, 2004.

Jackson, Jacqui. *Multicoloured Mayhem: Parenting the Many Shades of Adolescence, Autism, Asperger Syndrome and AD/HD.* London: Jessica Kingsley, 2004.

Jacobsen, Paula. *Asperger Syndrome and Psychotherapy: Understanding Asperger Perspectives.* London: Jessica Kingsley, 2003.

Kennedy, Diane M., with Rebecca Banks. *The ADHD-Autism Connection: A Step Toward More Accurate Diagnoses and Effective Treatments,* Colorado Springs, Colo.: WaterBrook Press, 2002.

Lawson, Wendy. *Build Your Own Life: A Self-Help Guide for Individuals With Asperger Syndrome.* London: Jessica Kingsley, 2003.

McCabe, Patrick, Estelle McCabe, and Jared McCabe. *Living and Loving with Asperger Syndrome: Family Viewpoints.* London: Jessica Kingsley, 2003.

Molloy, Harvey, and Latika Vasil. *Asperger Syndrome, Adolescence, and Identity: Looking Beyond the Label.* London: Jessica Kingsley, 2004.

Prior, Margot (ed.). *Learning and Behavior Problems in Asperger Syndrome.* New York: Guilford Press, 2003.

Stanford, Ashley. *Asperger Syndrome and Long-Term Relationships.* New York: Jessica Kingsley, 2003.

Szatmari, Peter. *A Mind Apart: Understanding Children with Autism and Asperger Syndrome.* New York: Guilford Press, 2004.

Willey, Liane Holliday (ed.). *Asperger Syndrome in Adolescence: Living with the Ups, the Downs and Things in Between.* London: Jessica Kingsley, 2003.

Winter, Matt. *Asperger Syndrome: What Teachers Need to Know.* London: Jessica Kingsley, 2003.

Index

Picture Credits

fotolia.com
        Etchison, Sonya: p. 81
        Kaulitzki, Sebastian: p. 24
        klosfoto: p. 61
        Krautberger, Gernot: p. 84
        krechet: p. 47
        Losevsky, Pavel: p. 82
        Mamluke, Nikolay: p. 50
        PhotoEuphoria: p. 66
        Pross, Richard: p. 23
        Spiro, Peter: p. 49
        StudioOne: p. 65
        Swanson, Lorraine: p. 112
        terrapanthera: p. 41
        Thompson, Leah-Anne: p. 39
Image Source: p. 42
istock.com
        Grotzinger Karen: p. 109
        Papantoniou, Antonis: p. 44
        Roorda, Audrey: p. 111
        Schmidt, Chris: p. 114
        Walicka, Ewa: p. 68
Jupiter Images: pp. 17, 18, 21, 28, 52, 62, 86, 94, 116
PhotoAlto
        O'Carroll, Patrick Sheándell: p. 26

To the best knowledge of the publisher, all other images are in the public domain. If any image has been inadvertently uncredited, please notify Harding House Publishing Service, Vestal, New York 13850, so that rectification can be made for future printings.

Authors

Zachary Chastain is a poetry editor currently living in Chicago, Illinois, where he is also continuing his education in English and communications. He has published numerous short stories and poems.

Phyllis Livingston has degrees in both psychology and special education. She has worked with many young adults who faced special challenges.

Series Consultants

Dr. Bridgemohan is an Assistant Professor in Pediatrics at Harvard Medical School and is a Board Certified Developmental-Behavioral Pediatrician on staff in the Developmental Medicine Center at Children's Hospital, Boston. She specializes in assessment and treatment of autism and developmental disorders in young children. Her clinical practice includes children and youth with autism, developmental language disorders, global delays, mental retardation, attentional and learning disorders, anxiety and depression. Dr. Bridgemohan is Co-director of residency training in Child Development at Children's Hospital, Boston, and is co-editor of "Bright Futures Case Studies for Primary Care Clinicians: Child Development and Behavior," a curriculum used nationwide in Pediatric Residency training programs. Dr. Bridgemohan has also published research and review articles on resident education, toilet training, autism screening and medical evaluation of children with developmental disorders.

Cindy Croft, M.A.Ed., is the Director of the Center for Inclusive Child Care (CICC) at Concordia University, St. Paul, MN. The CICC is a comprehensive resource network for promoting and supporting inclusive early childhood and school-age programs and providers with Project EXCEPTIONAL training and consultation, and other resources at www.inclusivechildcare. org. In addition to working with the CICC, Ms. Croft is faculty at Concordia University and Minneapolis Community and Technical College.